THE POSITIVE DICTIONARY

ONLY WORDS WITH POSITIVE MESSAGES

DR. PHIL MINNAAR

D0888222

EKSAL Quality Systems
Calgary
Canada

Published in Canada by EKSAL Quality Systems

Library and Archives Canada Cataloguing in Publication data

Minnaar Phil, 1940-

The positive dictionary: words with positive messages / Phil Minnaar.

Includes index.

ISBN: 0-9732042-1-4

1. Self-actualization (Psychology) — Dictionaries. 2. Happiness — Terminology — Dictionaries. 3. Mental Health — Dictionaries. I. Title.

BJ1456.M55 2006   158'.03   C2006-906128-9

Edited by Carmen Wittmeier
Printed in Canada by Bitzprint, Calgary
www.blitzprint.com

This book is dedicated to my wife, Adeline, for her support in my life; to my three children, Jerine, Eloise, and Phil; to their respective spouses, Jan, Tim, and Mari; and to our grandchildren, Adeline, Melinda, Renier, and Chelsea, all of whom gave me so much reason to be positive in life.

Thank you also to Carmen Wittmeier for her excellent editing.

Readers and users of *The Positive Dictionary* are encouraged to send comments to Phil Minnaar at philminn@shaw.ca or tel. (403) 247-1720.

Additional copies of *The Positive Dictionary* can be ordered by contacting Phil Minnaar at the e-mail address or telephone number shown above.

CONTENTS

FOREWORD

We are bombarded daily with negative news about events and trends. On a personal level we are also continuously subjected to stresses and worries. This tendency makes us more aware of the negatives in life than of the many good things. *The Positive Dictionary* can make a difference in this regard.

In this dictionary, the description of every word conveys a positive message. Each word is first used in the form of a positive action or activity which can be practiced on a daily basis. For every word there is also a basic truth in the form of a positive thought, a motto, or a slogan which can be followed in life. *The Positive Dictionary* covers the basic actions and values which ensure wellbeing in body, mind, and spirit, in associations with other people, and in the attainment of our goals.

You can use *The Positive Dictionary* to cultivate a positive outlook on life or to find inspiration in difficult times or when facing a major decision. You can look up a word to use in writing a letter or a card.

You can work systematically through the book by choosing specific words and deliberately putting them into action for a week or two or more. You can give *The Positive Dictionary* to family and friends as a gift to spread the message of positive living. You can donate *The Positive Dictionary* to people in dire situations to enable them to regain inspiration and confidence.

The Positive Pledge and the figure on the following two pages capture the essence of the book and can be used as general guiding principles for positive living.

It is my sincere belief that *The Positive Dictionary* will make a difference in your life. Use it. Practice its values, and life will become more radiant and positive.

Dr. Phil Minnaar

THE POSITIVE PLEDGE

I hereby pledge that I will:

- abide by the good values I have accepted;
- foster my spiritual life;
- be positive as a way of life;
- foster goodness;
- be pure and rational in my thinking;
- enjoy the many good things in life;
- care for my health and wellness;
- be courageous;
- be compassionate in my relationships;
- work diligently to get the best possible results;
- be effective in whatever I do;
- work to attain the goals I have set;
- continue to learn;
- be motivated in everything I do;
- and serve my community.

THE FIVE BASIC ELEMENTS OF POSITIVE LIVING

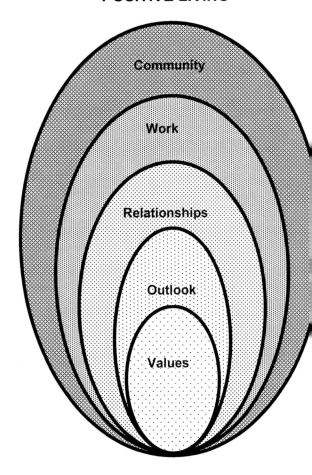

A

Abide: Abide by the values of honesty, decency, and trust.
- ❖ *To abide is to steer the course you have set for yourself.*

Ability: Develop your ability to think positively.
- ❖ *Ability empowers you to do the things you want to do.*

Able: Be able to do what you have set out to do.
- ❖ *To be able requires necessary knowledge and skills.*

Abolish: Abolish negativity and embrace the positive.
- ❖ *To abolish negativity requires will and determination.*

Aboveboard: Always plan and act aboveboard.
- ❖ *To be aboveboard and open is to be honest in all respects.*

Abreast: Keep abreast of the latest developments in your field.
❖ *Keeping abreast keeps you in the forefront.*

Absolute: Be in absolute control of your thoughts.
❖ *To maintain absolute control requires willpower and focus.*

Absolve: Absolve a person who has truly expressed regret.
❖ *Absolution clears the air and restores relationship.*

Absorb: Absorb knowledge about your field in order to perform your best.
❖ *To absorb knowledge is to build up a resource for practical use.*

Abstain: Abstain from everything that is detrimental to your wellbeing.
❖ *To abstain is to protect yourself from negative consequences.*

Accede: Accede when doing so will contribute to something good.
❖ *To accede is to recognize the merit of a request.*

Accept: Accept that success requires effort.
❖ *Acceptance clears the way for action.*

Accessible: Be accessible to people who need your advice or assistance.
❖ *Accessibility is an open door.*

Accommodate: Accommodate the diversity of people.
❖ *To accommodate is to accept the differences in people.*

Accord: Be in accord with views that conform to your values.
❖ *Accordance is an agreement to abide by certain principles.*

Accumulate: Accumulate books to read.
❖ *An accumulation of books becomes a library for reference.*

Accurate: Be accurate with the facts that you provide.
❖ *To be accurate is to do things right.*

Achieve: Achieve your goals through dedication and hard work.
- ❖ *Achievement is the outcome of focussed effort.*

Acknowledge: Acknowledge the good work of others.
- ❖ *Acknowledgement is to give credit where it is due.*

Acquaint: Acquaint yourself with the details of your task.
- ❖ *Acquaintance with details ensures better results.*

Acquiesce: Acquiesce to donate to a worthy cause.
- ❖ *Acquiescence is consenting to do something without complaint.*

Acquire: Acquire knowledge in diverse fields to become a rounded person.
- ❖ *Acquiring knowledge is an adventure of the mind.*

Act: Act in continuous pursuit of your goals.
- ❖ *To act is to translate your thoughts into results.*

Actuate: Actuate yourself and others to accomplish a task.
- ❖ *To actuate is to inspire and motivate.*

Acumen: Develop acumen in your field of work.
- ❖ *To have acumen is to be clever and ingenious.*

Acute: Be acute in solving problems.
- ❖ *An acute person is discerning, incisive, and smart.*

Adapt: Adapt to change while still preserving your principles.
- ❖ *Adaptation is a necessary adjustment in strategy.*

Adept: Be adept in your fields of interest.
- ❖ *To be adept is to be able and skilful.*

Adequate: Give adequate attention to all aspects of your task.
- ❖ *Adequate attention ensures adequate circumspection.*

Adhere: Adhere to your set goals in the face of resistance.
- ❖ *Adherence is a mark of persistence.*

Adjust: Adjust your strategies to overcome obstacles in your way.
* ❖ *An adjustment is a change in plans to reach your goals.*

Admire: Admire the good in others and accept that which is right.
* ❖ *Admiration is the recognition of the quality in others.*

Adopt: Adopt the ideas of others with proper acknowledgement.
* ❖ *The adoption of ideas expands the frontiers of development.*

Adore: Adore those who exemplify the good in people.
* ❖ *To adore is to admire and express goodwill towards others.*

Advance: Advance positive values in life.
* ❖ *Advancing something positive spreads the benefits to others.*

Adventurous: Be adventurous in your ventures.
* ❖ *An adventurous approach expands your boundaries.*

Advise: Advise others about the positive road to fulfilment.
❖ *To advise is to share your wisdom and experience.*

Advocate: Advocate the positive way of life.
❖ *To advocate is to be a champion of that in which you believe.*

Aesthetic: Cultivate an aesthetic appreciation for the finer things in life.
❖ *To be an aesthete is to be cultured and refined.*

Affable: Be affable to all people who come into contact with you.
❖ *Being affable, or good-natured and sociable, makes you approachable.*

Affect: Affect other people in a positive way.
❖ *To affect others is to embrace the opportunity to inspire.*

Affection: Radiate affection to your loved ones.
❖ *Affection forges closer bonds between people.*

Affiliate: Affiliate with those who make a difference.

❖ *Affiliation entails working together for something worthwhile.*

Affirm: Affirm your beliefs by stating them openly.

❖ *Affirming your beliefs demonstrates character.*

Aggregate: Aggregate knowledge about that which interests you.

❖ *To aggregate knowledge is to enrich your inner self.*

Agree: Agree only to that which is positive.

❖ *To agree requires careful thought and evaluation.*

Aim: Aim for the best in all you do.

❖ *To aim is to focus on your goal.*

Alacrity: Grab opportunities with alacrity.

❖ *To have alacrity is to be ready and eager to accept a challenge.*

Allay: Allay uneasiness in others.
❖ *Allaying uneasiness builds the confidence of others.*

Allegiance: Demonstrate allegiance to your country.
❖ *To have allegiance is to belong.*

Alleviate: Alleviate the burdens of others through positive actions.
❖ *Alleviating burdens brings relief to others.*

Alliance: Forge an alliance to work together for the good.
❖ *Alliances combine individual strengths into greater strength.*

Allot: Allot sufficient time for relaxation.
❖ *Allotting divides time into sensible proportions.*

Allure: Allure people around you.
❖ *To allure is to attract people with sincere charm and appeal.*

Almighty: Everything we plan to do is subject to the Will of the Almighty.

❖ *The Almighty determines our path but expects us to do our part.*

Altruistic: Practice altruistic behaviour as a habit.

❖ *Altruism is benevolent and considerate caring.*

Amass: Amass knowledge about your fields of interest, and success will follow.

❖ *To amass knowledge is to build a foundation for success.*

Ambition: Develop ambition to preserve and foster that which is good.

❖ *Ambition is a driving force to be channelled for the good.*

Amenable: Be amenable to suggestions.

❖ *To be amenable is to be willing to consider the opinions of others.*

Amend: Amend the negatives in your life.

❖ *Amending is the act of correcting that which is wrong.*

Amiable: Be amiable in all your interactions.
* ❖ *Amiable behaviour creates a friendly and pleasant atmosphere.*

Amuse: Amuse people without losing your dignity.
* ❖ *Amusement lightens burdens and creates entertainment.*

Animate: Animate your fellow workers to do their best.
* ❖ *Animation results in energetic inspiration.*

Anticipate: Anticipate probable events and trends in the future.
* ❖ *To anticipate reduces uncertainty about the future.*

Apologise: Apologise for something you did wrong.
* ❖ *Apologising is a display of greatness.*

Appearance: Ensure that you always have a neat appearance.
* ❖ *Your appearance affects the opinions that people have about you.*

Appease: Appease angry people to calm them down.

❖ *Appeasement creates conditions for sensible communication.*

Applaud: Applaud that which is good.

❖ *Applauding a person or group for some worthwhile achievement inspires them to do even better.*

Apply: Apply yourself to realise your dreams.

❖ *Applying yourself to your goals is the certain way to achieve results.*

Appraise: Appraise the correctness of every step you take in life.

❖ *Appraising measures your decisions against you values.*

Appreciate: Appreciate what people have done for you.

❖ *To show appreciation is to thank from the heart.*

Approbation: Grant your approbation where it is well deserved.

❖ *Approbation is the approval of something with merit.*

Approve: Approve of that which is good.
❖ *Approval signifies acceptance.*

Aptitude: Use your aptitudes to accomplish your aims.
❖ *An aptitude is a talent which has to be further developed and refined.*

Ardent: Be an ardent promoter of positive values.
❖ *An ardent approach is filled with enthusiasm.*

Arise: Arise in the morning with thanks in your heart and enthusiasm for the day ahead.
❖ *Arising is the start of new beginnings.*

Ascend: Ascend to high points in your life.
❖ *To ascend is to reach the summits of your achievements.*

Assert: Assert your commitment to positive living.
❖ *To assert is to affirm and to declare your convictions.*

Assiduous: Be assiduous until your goal has been attained.
* ❖ *To be assiduous is to be persistent.*

Assure: Assure people of your loyalty to them or to a cause.
* ❖ *Assurance is a confirmation of trust.*

Astute: Be astute when working for a cause.
* ❖ *To be astute is to be clever and perceptive.*

Atone: Atone whenever you know what you did was wrong.
* ❖ *To atone is to say "I am sorry."*

Attain: Attain the goals you have set for yourself.
* ❖ *To attain a goal is an important measure of success.*

Attention: Give attention to detail.
* ❖ *To give attention is to focus on and consider something specific.*

Attentive: Be attentive to everybody.
* ❖ *Attentiveness is considerate focusing on another person.*

Attitude: Foster a positive attitude towards life.

❖ *A positive attitude attracts positive returns.*

Attract: Attract people to you through friendliness and sincerity.

❖ *Attracting people to you expands your horizons.*

Auspicious: Create auspicious circumstances for success.

❖ *Auspicious circumstances are favourable and promising opportunities to advance.*

Avail: Avail yourself to help in your community.

❖ *Availing yourself involves offering your time, energy, and resources for a cause.*

Avow: Avow a shortcoming where necessary instead of covering it up.

❖ *To avow a fact is a sign of integrity.*

Award: Award a person with a gratuity for good service.

❖ *To award is to show satisfaction and appreciation.*

B

Beam: Beam as you recognize the fullness of life.
- ❖ *To beam is to share your joy with others.*

Beautify: Beautify your home.
- ❖ *To beautify your home is to create a place of warmth for family and visitors.*

Becoming: Be becoming in appearance and behaviour.
- ❖ *To be becoming is to be attractive and graceful.*

Befriend: Befriend strangers and draw them closer.
- ❖ *Befriending others widens your circles of friends.*

Begin: Begin a task with enthusiasm.
- ❖ *The beginning is the starting point for success.*

Believe: Believe in your dreams.
- ❖ *Believing translates dreams into reality.*

Benefactor: Be a benefactor for a cause in which you believe.

❖ *A benefactor contributes and donates to foster something good.*

Benefit: Contribute your talents to the benefit of your community.

❖ *A benefit is an advantage which leads to betterment.*

Benevolent: Be benevolent towards those in need.

❖ *Benevolence is an expression of compassion.*

Benign: Be benign in your association with others.

❖ *A benign attitude of grace and consideration radiates warmth.*

Bloom: Watch the flowers bloom.

❖ *To watch flowers bloom is to view the wonders of nature.*

Bold: Be bold, and fear will disappear.

❖ *Boldness ensures courage and daring.*

Bountiful: Enjoy the bountiful blessings in your life.

❖ *Bountiful blessings deserve ample appreciation.*

Brave: Be brave and courageous in times of adversity.

❖ *Bravery overcomes and makes you master of the situation.*

Brisk: Be brisk and energetic when tackling a task.

❖ *Briskness ensures efficient use of time.*

C

Calm: Be calm and composed in all situations.
- ❖ *Calmness is a sign of strength.*

Can: Always believe that you can.
- ❖ *To believe that you can makes the impossible possible.*

Capable: Be capable in what you have to do.
- ❖ *Capability requires a combination of knowledge, skill, and intelligence.*

Captivate: Captivate your audience's attention.
- ❖ *To captivate is to gain people's full attention.*

Care: Care for people, for nature, for the environment, and for all that needs attention.
- ❖ *Caring is action with compassion.*

Celebrate: Celebrate the goodness in life.
- ❖ *Celebration is an expression of joy and gratitude.*

Certainty: Create certainty through positive action.
❖ *Certainty creates peace of mind.*

Character: Display character in all your dealings with people.
❖ *To have character is to be a person with honour and integrity.*

Charitable: Support charitable organizations of your choice.
❖ *Charitable deeds help to meet a need.*

Charm: Be charming in a sincere way.
❖ *A charming person puts the other person first.*

Cheerful: Be cheerful about the many good things in your life.
❖ *Cheerfulness creates happiness.*

Cherish: Cherish small things given to you in friendship or in love.
❖ *To cherish is to value and appreciate something with special meaning to you.*

Circumspection: Practice circumspection in all your decisions.
❖ *Circumspection is the careful way of considering all aspects of a situation.*

Civil: Be civil and courteous to all people.
❖ *Civility is the hallmark of civilization.*

Clarity: Ensure clarity in your conversations and writings.
❖ *Clarity fosters understanding.*

Clean: Be clean in all your dealings.
❖ *A clean approach is testimony to decency and openness.*

Cogent: Provide cogent examples to support your point of view.
❖ *Cogent examples are compelling and convincing.*

Cogitate: Cogitate about a problem before deciding what to do.
❖ *To cogitate is to contemplate and ponder.*

Cognizant: Be cognizant of needs in your community.

❖ *To be cognizant is be conscious and aware of the dynamics of your environment.*

Commemorate: Commemorate a person or group who has done something worthwhile.

❖ *Commemorating is keeping a positive memory alive.*

Commence: Commence every undertaking with determination to finish it.

❖ *A commencement is a fresh start with new possibilities.*

Commend: Commend a person for an achievement.

❖ *To commend is to compliment and praise those who deserve it.*

Commit: Commit yourself to be positive.

❖ *A commitment is a contract with yourself.*

Compassion: Demonstrate compassion to those in poor health or dire circumstances.
❖ *Compassion is action with sympathy from the heart.*

Compatible: Be compatible with changing circumstances.
❖ *To be compatible is to adapt to new situations and to handle them well.*

Compensate: Compensate those who have provided a service to you.
❖ *Compensation is the reward for a service or work done well.*

Competence: Continue to improve your competence in whatever you do.
❖ *Competence is a gateway to success.*

Comply: Comply with laws, regulations, standards, and requirements.
❖ *To comply is to adhere to quality.*

Comport: Comport yourself in a dignified way in any company.
❖ *Proper comportment earns respect.*

Compose: Compose yourself when pressures rise.
* ❖ *Composure is a display of calmness.*

Comprehend: Concentrate in order to comprehend fully.
* ❖ *To comprehend is to understand the situation as a whole.*

Compromise: Compromise in a dispute only to the extent that your principles and integrity will allow.
* ❖ *A compromise is the meeting point between different opinions.*

Conceive: Conceive new ideas through imaginative thinking.
* ❖ *Everything created by man was first conceived as an idea.*

Concentrate: Concentrate by fixing your attention on the matter at hand.
* ❖ *Concentration focuses the mind.*

Conciliate: Conciliate an adversary by winning him/her over from hostility.
* ❖ *To conciliate is to bring a person onto your side.*

Concise: Be concise in your writings and conversations.

❖ *To be concise is to be to the point.*

Concord: Reach concord in all your dealings.

❖ *Concord brings agreement, peace, and harmony.*

Concur: Concur to agree without compromising your integrity.

❖ *Concurrence is the foundation for united action.*

Condolence: Express condolences to people who grieve.

❖ *A condolence is an expression of true sympathy.*

Condone: Condone, forgive, and forget a wrong done to you when remorse was shown.

❖ *To condone, where acceptable, is to lighten your heart.*

Conduce: Always strive to conduce towards results.

❖ *Conducing, or leaning towards results is a certain way to attain those results.*

Conduct: Express your positive values in your conduct.

❖ *Your conduct and behaviour is an expression of your inner self.*

Confident: Be confident that you can do what you have set out to do.

❖ *Confidence is the unwavering belief that you will succeed.*

Confirm: Confirm your belief in positive living.

❖ *To confirm is to express your approval and endorsement.*

Conform: Conform only to those norms which are right, honest, and durable.

❖ *Conforming to positive values is the basis of integrity.*

Confront: Confront those that spread negativity.

❖ *To confront is to stand up to a person with whom you disagree.*

Congenial: Be congenial with those close to you.

❖ *Congeniality is a demonstration of warmth and agreeability.*

Congratulate: Congratulate those who have achieved something worthwhile.

❖ *To congratulate is to recognize something well done.*

Connect: Connect with people who have positive values.

❖ *Your connections and associations determine your sphere of influence.*

Conquer: Conquer your fears.

❖ *To conquer is to overcome your fears by facing them.*

Conscience: Listen to your conscience and walk on the right side.

❖ *Your conscience is the watchdog in charge of your wellbeing.*

Conscientious: Be conscientious by doing things carefully, correctly, and faithfully.
❖ *Conscientiousness ensures quality results.*

Conscious: Be conscious of the abundance of good things in your life.
❖ *To be conscious is to be aware and to observe.*

Consent: Consent to something only when it conforms to your beliefs and values.
❖ *To consent is to agree to do something.*

Conserve: Conserve that which will otherwise go to waste and destruction.
❖ *Conserving is saving for future benefit.*

Consider: Consider all aspects of a matter before making a decision.
❖ *Considering the details leads to good decisions.*

Consistent: Be consistent in your approach to positive living.
❖ *Consistency is a persistent and steady conformance to your values.*

Console: Console and comfort those who have experienced a loss.
- ❖ *To console is to express true sympathy.*

Consonance: Promote consonance in your relationships with people.
- ❖ *Consonance is harmony and concord within groups.*

Construct: Construct something from basic parts to create a whole.
- ❖ *To construct is to create something real.*

Consult: Consult by asking advice from people who know.
- ❖ *To consult is to benefit from the wisdom of others.*

Contemplate: Contemplate how best to address a problem.
- ❖ *Contemplation brings clarity.*

Contingency: Handle contingencies in a calm and rational way.
- ❖ *A contingency is an emergency in which you can perform positively.*

Contribute: Contribute your knowledge, your money, and your time to a cause.
* *To contribute is to give a part of you.*

Convalesce: Convalesce from illness by thinking positively.
* *Convalescence can be fostered through a positive approach.*

Conviction: Stick to your convictions in all circumstances.
* *Your convictions consist of that in which you believe.*

Cooperate: Cooperate with others in working toward a goal.
* *Cooperation combines strengths to produce more strength.*

Cope: Cope with problems through a steadfast resolution to overcome them.
* *To cope is to be able to handle problems.*

Cordial: Be cordial to all around you.
* *Cordiality is a display of friendliness and sincerity.*

Correct: Be correct in your conduct.
- ❖ *Correct conduct involves behaviour that is acceptable and appropriate.*

Courage: Display courage in moments of danger.
- ❖ *To be courageous is to be brave and fearless.*

Courteous: Be courteous to everyone who crosses your path.
- ❖ *Courtesy is an expression of respect.*

Covenant: Create a covenant with yourself to pursue positive living.
- ❖ *A covenant is an agreement which should be kept.*

Create: Create new ideas, new things, and new relationships.
- ❖ *Creativity produces something that has never before existed.*

Credibility: Protect your credibility.
- ❖ *Your credibility is the extent to which people trust you.*

Cultivate: Cultivate your interests.
❖ *To cultivate something is to foster and promote that which is dear to you.*

Curious: Be curious about the fascinating world around you.
❖ *Curiosity leads to discoveries.*

Curtail: Curtail the temptation to become negative.
❖ *Curtailing keeps us from attitudes that will harm us.*

D

Dare: Dare yourself to do what you think is impossible.
❖ *To dare is to test your courage.*

Debate: Debate the good and the bad, and choose the good.
❖ *To debate is to discuss and to reach a conclusion.*

Debonair: Develop a debonair attitude.
❖ *A debonair attitude radiates buoyancy and elegance.*

Decent: Be decent in your behaviour.
❖ *To be decent is to behave appropriately and befitting.*

Decide: Decide after careful deliberation.
❖ *A decision creates certainty.*

Dedicate: Dedicate as much time as possible to fostering good causes.
❖ *To dedicate your time is an act of devotion.*

Deed: Do a good deed whenever you can.
❖ *A good deed is an act of compassion.*

Defeat: Defeat negativity.
❖ *To defeat is to conquer.*

Defend: Defend that which is right.
❖ *To defend is to stand up and protect all that is dear to you.*

Defray: Defray that which you owe.
❖ *To defray is to settle a debt.*

Defy: Defy those who treat you in a negative way.
❖ *To defy is to face opposition directly.*

Delectable: Arrange a delectable evening out.
❖ *A delectable, enjoyable evening at a play, an opera, a symphony, or whatever you choose nourishes the spirit.*

Delegate: Delegate responsibilities to those over whom you have authority.
❖ *To delegate is to trust that the responsibilities will be carried out.*

Deliberate: Be deliberate in your actions.
❖ *To be deliberate is to act with circumspection and consideration.*

Delicious: Enjoy a delicious meal.
❖ *Delicious food nourishes body and mind.*

Delight: Delight in the things that bring quality to life.
❖ *To delight is to express gladness.*

Demonstrate: Demonstrate your commitment to positive living.
❖ *A demonstration is evidence of your beliefs.*

Denounce: Denounce those things that detract from goodness.
❖ *To denounce or openly reject the bad is to stand up for the good.*

Depend: Depend on God for strength.
❖ *To depend is to believe and to trust.*

Derive: Derive pleasure from positive happenings.
❖ *To derive is to gain something good.*

Deserve: Be deserving of that for which you have strived and worked.
❖ *To deserve is to pick the fruits of dedication.*

Desire: Desire a life committed to positive living.
- ❖ *A strong desire will transform into reality.*

Desist: Desist from a bad habit.
- ❖ *To desist is to cease doing something that is unfruitful or unproductive.*

Determination: Be determined to accomplish your goal.
- ❖ *Determination is the driving force for success.*

Develop: Develop a positive attitude as a way of life.
- ❖ *Development causes growth and fulfillment.*

Devise: Devise new ways to make every day interesting.
- ❖ *To devise is to think and act creatively.*

Devote: Devote time and energy to building friendships.
- ❖ *Devotion is dedication to something that is important to you.*

Devout: Be devout in your duties.
* ❖ *To be devout is to be fully committed.*

Dexterous: Be dexterous in your activities.
* ❖ *To be dexterous is to be handy at doing practical things.*

Differentiate: Differentiate between good and bad.
* ❖ *To differentiate is to distinguish the good.*

Dignify: Dignify the good in others.
* ❖ *Dignity is the mark of respectability.*

Diplomatic: Be diplomatic in sensitive situations.
* ❖ *A diplomatic approach curbs animosity.*

Discern: Discern between that which is good and that which is bad.
* ❖ *To discern is to recognize the difference and to choose accordingly.*

Discourse: Seek opportunities to have a discourse on positive living.
❖ *Discourse is discussion with a purpose.*

Discover: Discover the beauty in your area.
❖ *Discovering beauty opens up new worlds around you.*

Discretion: Use your discretion to differentiate between good and bad.
❖ *Good discretion makes it easier to discern the good.*

Distinguish: Distinguish between the positive and the negative, and always choose the positive.
❖ *To distinguish is to ascertain the difference and choose the best option.*

Do: Do what you have to do.
❖ *Doing is a sure way to success.*

Donate: Donate your energy, time, and money to meet a need that is truly worthy.
❖ *A donation alleviates a need.*

Drive: Cultivate a drive to serve your community.
❖ *A drive is the initiative and motivation to accomplish a goal.*

Durable: Cultivate durable friendships.
❖ *Durable friendships are anchors in life.*

E

Eager: Be eager to help in the community when time permits.
❖ *Eagerness creates energy.*

Earn: Earn your income through honest, dedicated work.
❖ *Earning is receiving compensation for services rendered.*

Earnest: Be earnest in your commitment to positive living.
❖ *To be earnest is to be serious and determined.*

Ease: Ease a burden by facing and solving it.
❖ *To ease is to lighten a burden that weighs you down.*

Edify: Edify others in the things of which you are knowledgeable.
❖ *Edification enlightens and informs.*

Educate: Educate yourself in those things that are important for your work and life in general.
❖ *Education is the gateway to progress.*

Effect: Be conscious of the effect that you have on others.
❖ *Your effect on somebody should always be positive.*

Effective: Be effective in your undertakings.
❖ *Effectiveness is a measure of the extent to which goals are attained.*

Effervesce: Effervesce, and exude liveliness and energy.
❖ *Effervescence is the hallmark of excitement, exuberance, and enthusiasm.*

Efficient: Be efficient in your daily tasks.
❖ *Efficiency is a measure of what you produce with available resources.*

Elate: Elate someone with a compliment.
❖ *Elatedness is delight, joy, and jubilance about something good.*

Elect: Always elect the best option in order to reap positive results.
❖ *To elect is to choose between various possibilities.*

Elevate: Elevate people by lifting up and heartening them.
* ❖ *Elevation is the result of inspiration.*

Eliminate: Eliminate negative thoughts.
* ❖ *Eliminating negative thoughts cleanses the mind.*

Elude: Elude negative temptations.
* ❖ *To elude is to use your wits to avoid harmful influences.*

Embark: Embark on a new venture.
* ❖ *Embarking always creates a new beginning.*

Embolden: Embolden others to tackle the obstacles in their paths.
* ❖ *To be emboldening is to imbue others with courage.*

Embrace: Embrace that which has enduring value.
* ❖ *To embrace is to accept, adopt, and promote that in which you believe.*

Emotion: Employ positive emotions in your actions.

❖ *Positive emotions create drive and gusto.*

Empathy: Express and display empathy with people in distress.

❖ *Empathy is sympathy blended with compassion.*

Empower: Empower people with the knowledge and confidence needed to accomplish.

❖ *Empowering people lays the foundations for advancement.*

Emulate: Emulate people who achieve.

❖ *Emulating that which is good in people will make it a part of you.*

Enable: Enable people around you to accomplish their best.

❖ *Enabling others creates capability.*

Enact: Enact a positive attitude towards life.

❖ *To enact or put positive attitudes into practice will result in positive living.*

Enchanting: Be enchanting in your interrelationships.
❖ *To enchant is to captivate and delight.*

Encourage: Encourage people to use their talents.
❖ *Encouraging people expands their expectations of themselves.*

Endear: Endear yourself to those whom you love.
❖ *Endearment is a word or an act of genuine affection.*

Endeavour: Endeavour to approach every day with positivity.
❖ *To endeavour is to aspire to accomplish something specific.*

Endorse: Endorse the positive in life through positive actions.
❖ *To endorse is to approve of and promote something in which you believe.*

Endow: Endow money or resources to a worthwhile cause.
❖ *An endowment is a gift for the benefit of others.*

Endue: Endue people with good advice.
- ❖ *To endue is to provide in a time of need.*

Energy: Put energy into all of your endeavours.
- ❖ *Energy is the fire that fuels your actions.*

Enforce: Let your values be enforced through all your decisions.
- ❖ *To enforce is to reinforce that in which you believe.*

Engage: Engage people to become involved in service to the community.
- ❖ *To engage people is to enlist them for a cause.*

Enhance: Enhance a cause in which you believe.
- ❖ *To enhance is to improve and strengthen something worthwhile.*

Enjoy: Enjoy your accomplishments, your family and friends, and the humour in life.
- ❖ *Enjoyment is a spontaneous expression of happiness.*

Enlarge: Enlarge your circles of friends.
* *An enlarged circle of friends expands your world.*

Enlighten: Enlighten people by sharing your knowledge.
* *Enlightenment ensures growth in those around you.*

Enliven: Enliven your environment by being active and cheerful.
* *To enliven is to brighten and cheer up those around you.*

Enough: Be satisfied when you have enough for your purpose.
* *To have enough is to reach fulfillment.*

Enrapture: Be enraptured by good experiences.
* *To be enraptured is to derive intense pleasure from that which is good.*

Ensure: Ensure that what you do is right and good.
* *To ensure is to establish certainty.*

Enterprise: Be positive in all your enterprises.
❖ *An enterprise is an undertaking to reach a goal.*

Enthusiasm: Be enthusiastic about life, and life will be good to you.
❖ *Enthusiasm is contagious.*

Entrust: Entrust others with responsibilities.
❖ *To entrust is to believe in someone.*

Eradicate: Eradicate negative habits.
❖ *To eradicate is to eliminate completely.*

Establish: Establish something new that has never before existed.
❖ *Establishing is creating a new beginning.*

Esteem: Esteem those who have accomplished something good.
❖ *To have esteem for a person is to have a high regard for him or her.*

Evaluate: Evaluate by judging the value of something.

❖ *To evaluate is to assess the extent of something's quality.*

Evoke: Evoke enthusiasm in your daily life.

❖ *To evoke is to arouse self-motivation.*

Evolve: Evolve your projects through creative thinking.

❖ *Evolvement is growth through innovation.*

Exact: Be exact in whatever you do.

❖ *To be exact is to be true and unequivocal.*

Exalt: Exalt and applaud that which is good and right.

❖ *Exaltation is an acclamation of something worthwhile.*

Examine: Examine all aspects before making a decision.

❖ *To examine is to analyze and appraise.*

Example: Be an example in your community.
❖ *To be an example requires qualities that will inspire.*

Exceed: Exceed by going beyond the limits you have set for yourself.
❖ *To exceed is to expand your own boundaries.*

Excel: Excel by using your talents.
❖ *To excel is to be a master in your field.*

Excellent: Strive to be excellent in whatever you do.
❖ *Excellence is the mark of competence.*

Excite: Excite those around you to do their best.
❖ *Excitement creates energy.*

Exemplify: Exemplify your explanations with examples.
❖ *To exemplify is to be an example for others to follow.*

Exert: Exert your influence to convince others to embrace positive living.

❖ *To exert influence is to embrace the opportunity to spread the message of positive living.*

Extol: Extol the virtues of others by praising them.

❖ *To extol is to show admiration.*

Exuberance: Start every day with exuberance.

❖ *Exuberance is eagerness and enthusiasm about the opportunities of a new day.*

Exult: Exult upon overcoming obstacles and attaining your goals.

❖ *Exultation is the celebration of accomplishment.*

F

Fabulous: Strive to attain fabulous results.
❖ *Fabulous and astounding things happen because of positive living.*

Face: Face adverse situations head-on.
❖ *Facing a negative situation is a sign of character.*

Facilitate: Facilitate to assist progress.
❖ *To facilitate is to ensure that things run smoothly.*

Fair: Be fair in your opinions of people.
❖ *Fairness allows for human frailties.*

Faith: Have faith that you will prevail.
❖ *Faith is the foundation of success.*

Fascinate: Be fascinated by the wonders of nature.
❖ *To be fascinated about nature is to be captivated by its complexity and beauty.*

Felicitate: Felicitate people on their accomplishments.

❖ *A felicitation is a congratulation for something done well.*

Fidelity: Foster and protect your fidelity.

❖ *Fidelity entails faithful devotion to your duties, loyalty, and trustworthiness.*

Finish: Finish what you have started.

❖ *Three things finished are better than thirty left unfinished.*

Follow: Follow your goals with determination.

❖ *To follow a goal is to believe in yourself.*

Forbear: Forbear from those things that are detrimental to your health and wellbeing.

❖ *To forbear is to resist temptation.*

Forecast: Forecast future developments as accurately as possible.

❖ *Forecasting fosters preparedness.*

Foresee: Foresee the future.

❖ *Foresight is an anticipation of events that may happen.*

Form: Form habits that contribute to your wellbeing.

❖ *To form something is to establish it.*

Fresh: Adopt a fresh approach in every undertaking.

❖ *A fresh approach stimulates the creative mind.*

Frugal: Be frugal without being stingy.

❖ *Frugal living ensures future security.*

Fun: Have fun and enjoy life.

❖ *Fun lightens life's burdens.*

Function: Function in a positive way.

❖ *To function is to have the ability to act.*

Further: Further your causes and that in which you believe.

❖ *To further a cause is to work for something bigger than you.*

G

Gather: Gather a wide circle of friends around you.
- ❖ *Gathering circles of friends broadens your interactions.*

Gentle: Be gentle in how you treat people.
- ❖ *To be gentle is to be amiable and kind.*

Give: Give from your heart.
- ❖ *The more you give, the more you will receive.*

Good: Be good in everything you do.
- ❖ *To be good is to create more good in the world.*

Goodwill: Express goodwill to those who cross your path.
- ❖ *Spread goodwill, and goodwill will be returned.*

Grace: Act with grace.
- ❖ *To be gracious is to be compassionate and well-mannered.*

Grateful: Be grateful for what is bestowed on you.
❖ *Gratitude is a reflection of appreciation for what you have received.*

Gregarious: Be gregarious in social situations.
❖ *A gregarious person is companionable and outgoing.*

Gratuity: Give a gratuity for a service rendered.
❖ *A gratuity is a symbol of your gratitude.*

Guarantee: Guarantee that what you have done was done well.
❖ *To guarantee is to give your word.*

Guard: Guard all that is dear to you.
❖ *To guard is to protect the good in life.*

Gusto: Put gusto in everything you do.
❖ *Gusto combines enthusiasm with exhilaration.*

H

Habit: Work on eliminating a habit that detracts from positive living.
❖ *Habits are behavioural patterns that can always be improved.*

Handy: Be handy in whatever you do.
❖ *To be handy is to be adept and skilful in doing things.*

Hardy: Be hardy in times of hardship.
❖ *To be hardy is to be strong and resolute.*

Harmony: Create harmony in the groups with which you are dealing.
❖ *Harmony creates cohesion.*

Health: Care for your health.
❖ *Health is important in that it enables you to be active.*

Hearty: Be hearty, warm, and sincere.
❖ *A hearty, cheerful person attracts people.*

Heed: Heed that which is of value to you.
- ❖ *To heed is to pay attention and to care.*

Help: Help and assist those in need.
- ❖ *Helping is the action in caring.*

Heritage: Help to conserve your community's heritage.
- ❖ *Heritage is a historical and cultural treasure that must be saved.*

Heroic: Be heroic and courageous in order to preserve life.
- ❖ *A heroic deed is a courageous act of caring.*

Holistic: Use a holistic approach in your thinking.
- ❖ *A holistic approach covers all of the parts to form a whole.*

Homage: Pay homage to those whom you admire.
- ❖ *Homage is an acknowledgement of that which is great in people.*

Homey: Create a homey atmosphere in informal gatherings.
❖ *A homey atmosphere radiates warmth and friendliness.*

Honest: Be honest in all that you do and all that you say.
❖ *Honesty is a good and straight path in life.*

Honour: Protect your honour.
❖ *Your honour is based on your integrity, principles, and values.*

Hope: Hope that good things will come your way.
❖ *Hope is the longing for the realization of your desire.*

Humble: Be humble and unpretentious.
❖ *Humbleness is a characteristic of greatness.*

Humour: Cultivate a sense of humour.
❖ *Humour is the ability to see and enjoy the funny side of life.*

I

Ideal: Always set an ideal for your goals.
❖ *An ideal is a standard for which to strive.*

Illuminate: Illuminate the facts when you explain something.
❖ *To illuminate is to shed light on a subject.*

Imagine: Imagine the possibilities and act upon them.
❖ *Imagination is the wonderful ability of your mind to venture into the unknown.*

Impartial: Be impartial when judging a dispute or a competition.
❖ *Impartiality is a requirement for fairness in judging.*

Impeccable: Strive to deliver impeccable work.
❖ *Impeccable results are the hallmark of quality.*

Impress: Impress on people the importance of positive values.
❖ *To impress is to influence people to do what is right.*

Improve: Improve on a previous performance.
❖ *There is always potential for improvement.*

Incentive: Provide an incentive to inspire people to perform better.
❖ *An incentive is a driving force for improvement.*

Increase: Increase your monthly savings.
❖ *To increase savings is to enhance financial security.*

Induce: Induce people to be more positive.
❖ *To induce is to take an opportunity to influence people positively.*

Influence: Influence people for the better.
❖ *Influence is a powerful force to change people for the good.*

Inform: Inform others when good things happen to you.
- ❖ *Information about good things is uplifting.*

Infuse: Infuse a spirit of enthusiasm in a group.
- ❖ *The infusion of a positive spirit leads to positive results.*

Ingenious: Be ingenious when striving to create different ways of doing things.
- ❖ *To be ingenious is to create new possibilities.*

Initiate: Initiate new undertakings through careful planning and imagination.
- ❖ *Initiative is the act of starting on your own.*

Innovate: Innovate new products, methods, and procedures.
- ❖ *Innovation is the transformation of dreams into reality.*

Inspire: Inspire the people with whom you work to help you follow your dreams.
- ❖ *Inspiring people lights the fires of enthusiasm.*

Instil: Instil the importance of positive values in people around you.
❖ *Instilling is a means of promoting good values.*

Instinct: Use your instinct in adverse situations.
❖ *Instinct is that innate genius in your subconscious that compels you to do the right thing.*

Integrate: Integrate separate things into a single entity.
❖ *Integration creates a beneficial whole.*

Integrity: Ensure integrity in all your dealings with people.
❖ *Integrity is the hallmark of candour, honesty, and incorruptibility.*

Interest: Always learn more about things that interest you.
❖ *Interest is the spark that motivates you to acquire knowledge about something.*

Intrepid: Be intrepid in moments of danger.

❖ *Intrepidness is a sign of courage and boldness.*

Inure: Become inured in order to endure adverse situations.

❖ *To become inured requires toughening yourself over time.*

Invest: Invest time, energy, and money in a good cause.

❖ *Investment stimulates growth.*

Invigorate: Invigorate yourself through physical exercise.

❖ *Invigoration is to reenergize yourself with new enthusiasm.*

Invincible: Be invincible when protecting that which is good.

❖ *Invincibility is the absolute drive to fight for that which is good.*

Involve: Involve people in projects in your community.

❖ *To be involved in a group is to be part of a team.*

J

Joyful: Be joyful about all the good things in your life.
❖ *A joyful attitude is contagious.*

Jubilant: Be jubilant about very positive results.
❖ *Jubilation is the celebration of special achievements.*

Judgment: Be circumspective in your judgment of people.
❖ *Circumspection ensures fairness in judging people.*

Judicious: Be judicious when making decisions.
❖ *To be judicious is to show good judgement.*

Just: Be just in your dealings with people.
❖ *To be just is to be fair-minded, honest, and unbiased.*

K

Keen: Be keen to accept a new challenge.
- ❖ *To be keen is to be enthusiastic in tackling a new opportunity.*

Kind: Be kind and caring to all people and to all creatures of nature.
- ❖ *A kindness rendered makes the world a better place.*

Kindle: Kindle a positive spirit in others.
- ❖ *To kindle is to light a flame in people.*

Know: Acquire knowledge through constant learning.
- ❖ *The more we know, the more we know that there is so much more to know.*

Knowledge: Share your knowledge for the good.
- ❖ *Knowledge can be given away without being lost.*

L

Labour: Labour with dedication in pursuit of your goals.
❖ *A labour of love is enriching.*

Lasting: Cherish lasting memories of good things in your life.
❖ *Lasting memories are treasures to be remembered and shared.*

Laud: Laud God.
❖ *To laud or praise God is to know that we are dependent on the care of the Almighty.*

Laugh: Laugh about the funny and good things in life.
❖ *Laughter is healing.*

Launch: Launch your new project with enthusiasm.
❖ *Launching is the starting point of success.*

Lead: Lead by example.
❖ *Leadership is a quality which makes people long to follow you.*

Learn: Learn to become more knowledgeable and skilful.

❖ *Learning is the result of observing, processing, and storing that which is of interest to you.*

Leisure: Make time for leisure.

❖ *Leisure is a time for recuperation.*

Lenient: Be lenient and forgiving.

❖ *Leniency, where deserved, is an act of compassion.*

Lighten: Lighten the burden of those you love.

❖ *Lightening the burdens of others lifts their spirits.*

Live: Live to the fullest.

❖ *To live is to experience the wonders of creation.*

Lively: Act lively with enthusiasm.

❖ *Being lively spreads energy.*

Look: Always look on the bright side of situations.

❖ *Looking on the bright side can have such a transformative effect.*

Love: Love life, and life will be beautiful.
- ❖ *There is no greater power than the power of love.*

Lucid: Be lucid in your communication.
- ❖ *Lucid communication is clear, concise, and comprehensible.*

M

Magnificent: Appreciate the magnificent wonders of nature.
❖ *The magnificence and splendour of nature is endless in its variety.*

Maintain: Maintain what you have to keep it in good condition.
❖ *Maintenance prevents decay.*

Make: Make your dreams come true.
❖ *Taking the necessary risks and steps makes your dreams happen.*

Manifest: Let your values be manifest in your behaviour.
❖ *The manifestation of your values is there for everyone to see.*

Manners: Always display good manners.
❖ *Good manners are a sign of civility.*

Marvellous: Create opportunities for marvellous experiences.
❖ *A marvellous experience creates excitement and pleasure.*

Mediate: Mediate between those that disagree to bring about conciliation.
❖ *Mediation is a gateway to cooperation.*

Meditate: Meditate and consider carefully before making that important decision.
❖ *Meditation brings clarity and vision.*

Memorize: Memorize the key facts about the task at hand.
❖ *Memorizing creates a storehouse of knowledge.*

Memory: Develop your memory.
❖ *A good memory requires concentrated focus.*

Merit: Acknowledge the merits in people and award accordingly.
❖ *A merit is a characteristic of quality.*

Merriment: Bring some merriment into your daily life.
❖ *Merriment releases tension.*

Meticulous: Be meticulous without going overboard.
❖ *A meticulous approach ensures correctness.*

Mettle: Display mettle in tough situations.
❖ *To have mettle is to be bold, courageous, and daring.*

Mild: Be mild in your relationships with people while maintaining their respect.
❖ *Mildness softens aggression.*

Mind: Apply your mind to its full potential.
❖ *Your mind is the powerhouse of your whole being.*

Mission: Define your mission clearly and strive to fulfil it.
❖ *A mission gives direction to your life.*

Mitigate: Mitigate somebody's grief with compassion.
❖ *Mitigation lightens a burden.*

Moderate: Be moderate in all your interrelationships.

❖ *Moderation is the golden mean between extremes.*

Morale: Boost your morale through self-motivation.

❖ *A high morale enables you to do the extraordinary.*

Motivate: Motivate people to give their best.

❖ *Motivation is the driving force behind results.*

N

Natty: Be natty in how you dress.
* ❖ *To be natty is to be elegant.*

Navigate: Navigate through obstacles on your way to success.
* ❖ *To navigate is to plan and steer to reach your goal.*

Neat: Be neat in your appearance.
* ❖ *Neatness is a sign of self-confidence.*

Negotiate: Negotiate the best possible benefits.
* ❖ *To negotiate is to bargain for positive results.*

Noble: Follow noble goals in your community.
* ❖ *A noble goal represents that which is virtuous and worthy.*

Noteworthy: Strive towards noteworthy accomplishments.
* ❖ *A noteworthy accomplishment is an extraordinary and outstanding achievement.*

O

Obey: Obey your conscience.
- ❖ *Obedience to your conscience keeps you from straying into negative areas.*

Oblige: Oblige any reasonable request.
- ❖ *An obligation is a promise that has to be fulfilled.*

Observe: Observe your environment with curiosity.
- ❖ *Observation helps you notice the wonders of the world.*

Obtain: Obtain experience in the advantages of positive living.
- ❖ *To obtain is to acquire that which we need.*

Open: Open your mind to the wonderful world of books.
- ❖ *An open mind embraces new ideas.*

Opportunity: Take every opportunity to render a service.
- ❖ *An opportunity is a moment in time when circumstances are right for you to act.*

Optimum: Make optimum use of available resources.
* ❖ *The optimum is the maximum in effectiveness.*

Organize: Organize your life in order to be effective.
* ❖ *Being organized ensures optimum use of time.*

Original: Be original in whatever you do.
* ❖ *Originality enriches the world through the new possibilities it creates.*

Outcome: Ensure quality outcomes in your projects.
* ❖ *Quality outcomes have long-term quality effects.*

Outdo: Outdo the goals you have set for yourself.
* ❖ *To outdo is to surpass your expectations.*

Output: Maximize your output.
* ❖ *Output is the end result of your endeavours.*

Outset: At the outset, know where you are going.
❖ *The outset is the beginning of a new journey.*

Ovation: Give an ovation to celebrate someone's achievement.
❖ *An ovation is an occasion to pay homage.*

Overcome: Overcome the obstacles blocking the path to your goals.
❖ *To overcome is to triumph.*

Overjoyed: Be overjoyed about that which is especially good in your life.
❖ *To be overjoyed is to experience happiness in the extreme.*

P

Pacify: Pacify when emotions run high.
❖ *To pacify is to bring calmness and harmony.*

Partnership: Forge a partnership to accomplish your vision.
❖ *A partnership is the basis for cooperation.*

Passionate: Be passionate about your beliefs, your goals, your plans, and your life.
❖ *Passion is the expression of the inner force that drives you.*

Patron: Be a patron for the causes in which you believe.
❖ *A patron protects, upholds, and supports causes to the benefit of others.*

Pay: Pay what you owe.
❖ *To pay is to compensate for a service or a product delivered at your request.*

Peaceful: Make time to be peaceful.
❖ *Being peaceful lifts the spirit to reflect on the higher plains of life.*

Penchant: Develop a penchant for positive recreational activities.
❖ *A penchant is an inclination towards something specific.*

Pensive: Be pensive when you have to make an important decision.
❖ *Being pensive, or allowing time for deep thought, ensures clearer thinking.*

Perceive: Perceive people with objectivity.
❖ *A perception of a person is a judgement on our part.*

Perform: Perform in the most effective way possible.
❖ *To perform is to carry out your duties.*

Persevere: Persevere in times of hardship.
❖ *Perseverance is the will to keep on and overcome the adversities in life.*

Persist: Persist in following your goals.
❖ *Persistence paves the way to attaining your goals.*

Persuade: Persuade people to embrace positive living.
❖ *To persuade is to induce people to follow your advice and example.*

Peruse: Peruse your reading materials with care.
❖ *Perusing with care is the right way to absorb the essentials.*

Philanthropic: Be philanthropic by giving.
❖ *Philanthropy is the practical side of caring for fellow human beings.*

Plan: Plan ahead in all respects.
❖ *Planning shapes the future.*

Plausible: Always formulate plausible explanations.
❖ *Plausible explanations are persuasive and believable.*

Pleasant: Be pleasant in every gathering.
❖ *A pleasant person attracts people.*

Please: Please those whom you love with gifts of affection.
❖ *Pleasing creates happiness.*

Pleasure: Enjoy the pleasure of sharing.
❖ *It is a pleasure to see appreciation for something you did.*

Pledge: Honour your pledges.
❖ *A pledge is a promise which must be kept.*

Ply: Ply steadily in your work.
❖ *Plying is working diligently to reach your goals.*

Polished: Develop a polished style.
❖ *A polished style demonstrates elegance and grace.*

Positive: Be positive about everything in life, and life will treat you positively.
❖ *A positive attitude causes positive things to happen.*

Posture: Display a positive posture.
❖ *A positive posture or attitude conveys confidence and strength.*

Practical: Be practical in what you do.
* ❖ *To be practical is to be functional and down-to-earth.*

Pragmatic: Be pragmatic in whatever you do.
* ❖ *To be pragmatic is to be practical and realistic.*

Praise: Praise those who have achieved something, no matter how small.
* ❖ *Praising people is an act of admiration and encouragement.*

Praiseworthy: Strive to attain praiseworthy results.
* ❖ *To be praiseworthy requires excellence and quality.*

Pray: Pray every day with thankfulness.
* ❖ *To pray is to praise God and to receive strength.*

Precious: Cherish that which is precious to you.
* ❖ *A precious possession has personal value to you.*

Prepare: Prepare carefully for that future event.
❖ *Good preparation ensures success.*

Present: Give a present as a symbol of appreciation and thankfulness.
❖ *To give a present is to give from the heart.*

Presentable: Be presentable in your appearance on all occasions.
❖ *Being presentable is showing respect for other people.*

Prevail: Prevail under all circumstances.
❖ *To prevail is to persist and overcome obstacles in your path.*

Privilege: Appreciate any privilege provided to you and make the best of it.
❖ *A privilege is a unique opportunity not granted to many.*

Proactive: Be proactive to prevent negative events.
❖ *To be proactive is to foresee the future and act in anticipation.*

Procure: Procure the resources needed to attain your goals.

❖ *Procuring the necessities takes you one step closer to the achievement of your goals.*

Produce: Produce the results you hope to achieve.

❖ *A product of your mind or your hands is the fruit of your endeavours.*

Proficient: Be proficient and get results.

❖ *To be proficient is to use your knowledge, skills, and talents in an optimum way.*

Profuse: Show profuse kindness to those in need.

❖ *Giving profusely is the ultimate in caring.*

Progress: Progress along your chosen path.

❖ *Progress only comes through well-planned effort.*

Prolific: Be prolific in your output.

❖ *A prolific and abundant output is the result of dedicated effort.*

Promise: Fulfill your promise to help where necessary.

❖ *A promise is as good as a contract.*

Promote: Promote a cause in which you believe.

❖ *Promoting a cause ensures advancement.*

Propagate: Propagate the possibilities of positive living.

❖ *To propagate is to spread and foster a message.*

Proper: Act in a proper way according to your values.

❖ *Doing things properly is a guarantee of integrity.*

Propitious: Be propitious in respect to worthy causes.

❖ *To be propitious is to be favourably inclined towards people's ideas and requests.*

Prosper: Prosper by doing your best.

❖ *To prosper is to receive from what you have given.*

Provide: Provide for the future.
❖ *To set aside provisions is to exercise your foresight.*

Prowess: Exercise your prowess in everything you do.
❖ *Prowess combines aptitude with the ability to be effective.*

Prudent: Be prudent and save for the future.
❖ *Prudence requires discretion and farsightedness.*

Punctual: Be punctual at every meeting, without exception.
❖ *Arriving on time is a sign of respect for the time of others.*

Pure: Be pure in your thoughts.
❖ *Purity in thought excludes the negativities of our day and age.*

Purpose: Define your purpose in every task that you start.
❖ *A clearly defined purpose provides guidance from beginning to end.*

Pursue: Pursue the advantages of positive living.

❖ *To pursue is to seek and persist in that which is good.*

Q

Qualify: Qualify yourself for your tasks through diligent study and observation.
❖ *To be qualified is to be able to produce quality results.*

Quality: Ensure quality in all your outputs.
❖ *Quality is conformance with standards.*

Quest: Make a quest of your search for the truth.
❖ *A quest is a passionate search for answers.*

Quiet: Schedule time for quiet moments.
❖ *Quiet moments refresh body, mind, and spirit.*

R

Raise: Raise awareness of the benefits of positive living.
❖ *To raise awareness is to foster understanding.*

Rapture: Revel in feelings of rapture when especially good things occur.
❖ *To experience rapture is to feel extraordinary joy.*

Rational: Be rational in everything you do.
❖ *Rational thinking and behaviour is based on reality.*

Ready: Be ready for the unexpected.
❖ *To be ready is to be prepared.*

Realize: Realize your goals through dedicated work and effort.
❖ *To realize dreams is to bring them to fulfilment.*

Reap: Reap the benefits of positive living.
❖ *To reap is to harvest what was cultivated.*

Reason: Carefully reason through all of the implications of something you want to do.

❖ *Reasoning is the power of your mind to think.*

Reasonable: Be reasonable in your judgements.

❖ *Reasonable judgements are logical, sensible, and well thought out.*

Reassure: Reassure people continuously of your commitment and support.

❖ *Reassurance encourages and restores confidence.*

Rebound: Rebound whenever there is a setback.

❖ *To rebound is to refuse to give up.*

Receive: Receive with grace.

❖ *Receiving something is always enriching.*

Reciprocate: Reciprocate kindness received by giving kindness.

❖ *Reciprocation is giving back in equal measure.*

Recognize: Recognize the good in others.
❖ *Recognizing others is an expression of appreciation.*

Recollect: Recollect continuously the memories of good things that have happened to you.
❖ *A recollection of something good is a treasure to be preserved.*

Recommend: Recommend positive action to those who need it.
❖ *Recommending provides an opportunity to instil positive ideas.*

Reconcile: Reconcile differences in opinions.
❖ *Reconciliation creates mutual understanding.*

Reconsider: Reconsider previous decisions when circumstances have changed.
❖ *To reconsider is to adjust your strategy to ensure that your goals will still be attained.*

Recover: Recover from a setback with vigour and vision.

❖ *Recovery is the only way to rebound and go for those goals.*

Recreate: Recreate regularly to keep balanced.

❖ *Recreation recharges body, mind, and spirit with new vigour.*

Rectify: Rectify an error that has occurred, and be honest about it.

❖ *To rectify is to acknowledge that an error was made and to avoid hiding it.*

Redeem: Redeem that which may have caused harm to others.

❖ *To redeem is to make amends for something unfortunate that happened.*

Rediscover: Rediscover the lessons learned from earlier experiences.

❖ *Rediscovering is an exploration of hidden treasures.*

Redress: Redress that which caused distress to other people.

❖ *Redressing is the correction of a wrong.*

Reduce: Reduce your stress through positive activities.
❖ *Reducing stress creates new energy.*

Refine: Refine your manners.
❖ *To refine is to improve and polish your behaviour.*

Reform: Reform systems and procedures that are faulty and outdated.
❖ *Reform leads to renewal and improvement.*

Refrain: Refrain from that which is detrimental.
❖ *Refraining prevents you from deviating and getting side-tracked.*

Refresh: Refresh yourself after strenuous activity.
❖ *To refresh is to renew your strength.*

Regard: Regard people highly because of their special qualities.
❖ *Regard for other people is a sign of respect.*

Regenerate: Regenerate your projects through a renewed focus on your goals.

❖ *Regeneration is to breathe new life into projects that have stagnated.*

Rehabilitate: Rehabilitate that which has broken down.

❖ *To rehabilitate is to restore something to its original state.*

Rehearse: Rehearse your presentations.

❖ *Rehearsing beforehand ensures a better result.*

Reinforce: Reinforce your opinions with lucid arguments.

❖ *Reinforcement strengthens an impression.*

Rejoice: Rejoice every day about some good thing that will happen.

❖ *To rejoice is to be glad.*

Rejuvenate: Rejuvenate your spirit to attain new energy and vision.

❖ *Rejuvenation is a renewal of the spirit.*

Relax: Relax to regain strength and perspective.
* ❖ *Relaxation is the basis for rejuvenation.*

Relentless: Be relentless in protecting that which is good.
* ❖ *A relentless attitude flows from firm convictions.*

Reliable: Be reliable in your work and in all your dealings with people.
* ❖ *Reliability is the foundation of trust.*

Relieve: Relieve the stress of others.
* ❖ *To relieve is to offer the helping hand of compassion.*

Relish: Relish the excitement of an upcoming event.
* ❖ *To relish is to look forward to something positive.*

Rely: Rely on people to give their best.
* ❖ *To rely on people is to trust them.*

Remarkable: Strive to create remarkable achievements for the benefit of others.
* ❖ *A remarkable achievement is always the result of dedicated hard work.*

Remember: Remember those who have done good things for you.
* ❖ *Remembering good deeds keeps appreciation alive.*

Render: Render a service to your community.
* ❖ *To render a service is to make yourself available.*

Renew: Renew friendships that have waned over time.
* ❖ *Renewing friendships draws them closer.*

Renovate: Renovate that which has deteriorated over time.
* ❖ *Renovation restores and preserves for the future.*

Reorganize: Reorganize to adjust to changed circumstances.
* ❖ *Reorganization improves effectiveness.*

Repair: Repair that which has broken or needs renewal.
- ❖ *To repair is to restore something to its former state.*

Repay: Repay those who have shown kindness to you with more kindness.
- ❖ *Repaying is compensation in exchange.*

Repent: Repent when you feel sorry for something you have done wrong.
- ❖ *To repent is to regret and to atone for what was wrong on your side.*

Replenish: Replenish your resources.
- ❖ *To replenish is to replace that which has been used before it is needed again.*

Repose: Repose from time to time.
- ❖ *Repose, and the relaxation will recuperate your body.*

Represent: Represent, or embody, the positive way of living.
- ❖ *To represent is to be an example.*

Reputation: Build and protect your reputation as a person of honour.
* ❖ *Your reputation is how people see you as a person.*

Require: Require quality in everything you buy.
* ❖ *To require is to set your standards.*

Requite: Requite goodwill with goodwill.
* ❖ *Requiting is the repaying for something received.*

Resolute: Be resolute in attaining your goals.
* ❖ *To be resolute is to be determined to reach those goals, regardless of obstacles.*

Resolve: Resolve to be positive in all matters.
* ❖ *To resolve is to make a firm decision and adhere to it.*

Resourceful: Be resourceful in whatever you do.
* ❖ *Resourcefulness is finding the best way of doing things.*

Respectable: Be respectable in your conduct and appearance.
❖ *Respectability is a measure of the image that people have of you.*

Respectful: Be respectful to all people, regardless of position or origin.
❖ *Respect is a mark of honour.*

Restful: Be restful at times to restore your energy.
❖ *A restful and peaceful hour is time well spent.*

Restore: Restore your energy by resting peacefully.
❖ *Restoration prepares you for renewed activity.*

Restrain: Restrain yourself when irritated.
❖ *Restraining yourself prevents you from responding in a negative way.*

Result: Be proud of the result obtained through your honest, hard work.
❖ *A result is the end product of dreaming, planning, and doing.*

Retain: Retain that which is good.
❖ *To retain is to keep and save.*

Retrieve: Retrieve those good things which may have been neglected for some time.
❖ *To retrieve is to find again.*

Revel: Revel in your accomplishments.
❖ *To revel is to take delight in achievements.*

Revere: Revere the positive values in life.
❖ *To revere something is to think highly of it.*

Revise: Revise your plans to adjust to new circumstances.
❖ *To revise is to be proactive.*

Revive: Revive those dreams yet to be fulfilled.
❖ *To revive is to bring things back to life.*

Reward: Reward those who have rendered a service to you.
❖ *A reward is a token of appreciation.*

Right: Make sure that you are right before you act.

❖ *To be right requires constant testing of your actions against your accepted values.*

Rise: Let your expectations of yourself rise continuously.

❖ *To allow your expectations to rise is to motivate yourself to develop and grow.*

Rollick: Have a rollicking celebration with others.

❖ *A rollick is a jovial and merry occasion.*

Romance: Be romantic at times in your dreams and imagination.

❖ *To be romantic is to dream idealistically with no practical limitations.*

S

Sacrifice: Sacrifice something if it will lead to a greater good.
❖ *To sacrifice is to offer something dear to you.*

Sagacious: Be sagacious in solving problems.
❖ *Sagaciousness is a demonstration of cleverness and good judgement.*

Salubrious: Create salubrious conditions and habits for a healthy life.
❖ *A salubrious life is wholesome for body, mind, and soul.*

Salutation: Be warm and honest in your salutations.
❖ *A salutation is a welcome greeting.*

Salve: Salve the physical, mental, and spiritual wounds of others.
❖ *To salve is to soothe the pain of those for whom you care.*

Satisfy: Be satisfied that what you are doing is the right thing to do.
❖ *Satisfy yourself by using your values as a measure.*

Save: Save for the future.
❖ *To save is to put away extra for possible times of need.*

Scholar: Be a scholar through constant study.
❖ *A scholar continues to delve into ever deeper levels of knowledge.*

Secure: Be secure in the good values you are following.
❖ *To be secure is to be confident and assured.*

Sedulous: Be sedulous in your work.
❖ *A sedulous attitude is one that is industrious and diligent.*

Self-confidence: Maintain your self-confidence by always believing in yourself.
❖ *Self-confidence is a requirement for success.*

Self-control: Exercise self-control in difficult situations.
❖ *Self-control is a powerful force that keeps you in control of your thoughts and actions.*

Self-esteem: Foster a positive self-esteem.
❖ *Self-esteem is how you see yourself.*

Self-possessed: Be self-possessed in your interactions with people.
❖ *To be self-possessed is to be calm, poised, and self-assured.*

Self-reliant: Be self-reliant in whatever you do.
❖ *Self-reliance depends on your belief that you can do it.*

Self-respect: Always guard your self-respect.
❖ *Self-respect is a measure of how you regard yourself.*

Self-restraint: Exercise self-restraint in adverse situations.
❖ *Self-restraint requires self-control.*

Self-sacrifice: Exercise self-sacrifice for those loved ones in need.
❖ *Self-sacrifice involves ignoring self-interest.*

Self-supporting: Be self-supporting.
❖ *Self-support is the result of diligence and hard work.*

Sensible: Be sensible in all your decisions.
❖ *Sensible decisions are the result of common sense.*

Sensitive: Be sensitive to avoid hurting others.
❖ *Sensitivity entails consideration of another person's feelings.*

Sentimental: Be sentimental about small memorabilia.
❖ *To be sentimental is to cherish the memories rekindled by memorabilia.*

Serve: Serve your country in any way you can.
❖ *To serve your country is to give in return.*

Shape: Let positive things shape your life.
❖ *To be shaped by positive things leads to positive living.*

Shield: Shield those you love against injury and distress.
❖ *To shield is to put yourself between a loved one and imminent harm.*

Side: Walk on the side of goodness.
❖ *The side of goodness preserves the values of positive living.*

Sincere: Always be sincere in what you say and what you do.
❖ *Sincerity breaks down barriers.*

Skilful: Be skilful in solving problems.
❖ *Skill is a combination of knowledge and ability.*

Sobriety: Make sobriety one of your basic principles.
❖ *Sobriety is freedom from addiction.*

Solace: Find solace in times of sorrow.
❖ *Solace is the alleviation and relief from sadness.*

Solitude: Seek solitude to reflect on decisions to be made.

❖ *Solitude prevents distractions.*

Solve: Solve problem situations in the best possible way.

❖ *A solution is a well-thought-out answer to a problem.*

Soothe: Soothe the pain of loved ones with compassion.

❖ *Soothing is an expression of caring.*

Sorry: Say 'sorry' when there is reason to do so.

❖ *Saying 'sorry' is a sign of greatness.*

Sound: Obtain a sound understanding of whatever you undertake.

❖ *A sound understanding fosters quality results.*

Sparkle: Start the day with a sparkle in the eye.

❖ *A sparkle in the eye is a sign of vitality.*

Special: Be a special friend to those for whom you care.

❖ *To be special is to be true in all respects.*

Spirit: Kindle the spirit of goodwill wherever you go.

❖ *A spirit of goodwill creates positive results.*

Spirited: Be spirited in following your dreams.

❖ *High spirits reflect enthusiasm.*

Splendid: Strive towards splendid results in all your projects.

❖ *Splendid results are outstanding and admirable.*

Spread: Spread the message of positive living.

❖ *To spread a message is to advance a cause.*

Spring: Spring to life in the early morning.

❖ *Begin each day with vigour and eagerness.*

Spry: Be spry and results will follow.
❖ *To be spry is to be agile, brisk, and sprightly.*

Stalwart: Be stalwart in the pursuit of a cause.
❖ *A stalwart is courageous in defending a cause.*

Stamina: Use your stamina to maintain strength and endurance.
❖ *Stamina is the staying power to reach set goals.*

Stand: Take a stand for that in which you believe.
❖ *A stand is an expression of your convictions, regardless of opposition.*

Standard: Always strive to maintain a standard of excellence.
❖ *A standard is a measurement of quality.*

Staunch: Be a staunch friend to each of those you call a friend.
❖ *A staunch friend remains true in all circumstances.*

Steadfast: Be steadfast about your principles.

❖ *A steadfast attitude ensures that you remain on course.*

Steady: Be steady in pursuit of your goals.

❖ *To be steady is to stay on course in the pursuit of your goals.*

Stimulate: Stimulate others to follow common goals.

❖ *To stimulate is to light the fires of enthusiasm in others.*

Stoic: Be stoic in times of real pain.

❖ *A stoic attitude can enable you to bear severe pain and suffering.*

Strive: Always strive towards goals that will be of benefit to your fellow human beings.

❖ *To strive is to have something to live for.*

Strong: Be strong in body, mind, and spirit.

❖ *Strength helps conquer the impediments in life.*

Studious: Be studious in your daily tasks.
❖ *A studious approach will bear fruit.*

Study: Study all the facts relating to your work.
❖ *Diligent study results in expertise.*

Sublime: Seek the sublime.
❖ *The sublime is that which is lofty and noble.*

Success: Make success your life's ambition.
❖ *Success is reaching a goal, no matter how small.*

Sufficient: Ensure that you have the sufficient resources needed to achieve your goals.
❖ *Sufficient resources will enable you to meet requirements.*

Suggest: Suggest ways to do good things.
❖ *To suggest is to advise with good intentions.*

Sunny: Display a sunny disposition.
❖ *A sunny attitude is contagious.*

Superlative: Strive for the superlative in whatever you do.

❖ *Superlative results are of the highest quality.*

Sure: Be sure about the future success of your endeavours.

❖ *To be sure is to be confident.*

Surpass: Surpass the limits of what you think you can do.

❖ *To surpass is to exceed your own expectations.*

Surplus: Save a surplus for future use.

❖ *A surplus is that extra output which ensures growth.*

Surprise: Surprise those around you with things that make them feel good.

❖ *A surprise is an unforeseen pleasure.*

Survive: Survive adversity with resoluteness.

❖ *Survival is a hallmark of toughness.*

Sustain: Sustain your spirit of goodwill.

❖ *To sustain is to keep on going.*

Swift: Be swift to avoid a problem.

❖ *A swift response prevents catastrophes.*

Sympathy: Show sympathy to people in distress.

❖ *Sympathy is an expression of compassion.*

T

Tackle: Tackle every task with gusto.
* ❖ *To tackle is to begin and embark upon a task with enthusiasm.*

Tact: Act with tact.
* ❖ *To be tactful is to be considerate and polite.*

Talent: Use your talents to accomplish worthwhile goals.
* ❖ *A talent is a gift to be used for the good of mankind.*

Teach: Teach others the fundamentals of good living.
* ❖ *Teaching is the sharing of knowledge.*

Temperance: Exercise temperance in your behaviour.
* ❖ *Temperance is the avoidance of extremes.*

Tender: Be tender towards those close to you.
* ❖ *Tenderness is a manifestation of love.*

Terrific: Enjoy terrific vacations after strenuous work.

❖ *A terrific vacation rejuvenates the spirit.*

Thorough: Be thorough in everything you do.

❖ *Thoroughness is a guarantee of accuracy and dependability.*

Thoughtful: Be thoughtful through small acts of kindness.

❖ *Thoughtfulness entails doing little things to please somebody.*

Thrifty: Be thrifty and save.

❖ *Thriftiness leads to prosperity.*

Thrive: Thrive from your dedicated, hard work.

❖ *To thrive is to prosper.*

Tolerate: Tolerate up to a point before taking action.

❖ *Tolerance makes room for human weakness only to a certain degree.*

Toughen: Toughen your resolve to attain your goals.

❖ *To toughen yourself is to become strong enough to overcome the obstacles.*

Transcendent: Accomplish transcendent achievements.

❖ *A transcendent achievement is extraordinary.*

Transform: Transform that which is out-of-date into something effective and efficient.

❖ *A transformation creates new energy and focus.*

Treat: Treat other people with kindness and compassion.

❖ *How you treat people determines how they treat you.*

Tribute: Pay tribute to worthy achievements.

❖ *A tribute is recognition of something exceptional.*

Truce: Create a truce between adversaries.

❖ *A truce opens the way to mutual understanding.*

Trust: Trust the people working for you.
❖ *Trust is a motion of confidence.*

Truth: Constantly search for the truth.
❖ *The truth is a fact over which there is no dispute.*

Truthful: Be truthful in everything you do.
❖ *Truthfulness is the ultimate form of openness.*

U

Understand: Understand why people behave in certain ways.
* ❖ *Understanding creates bridges between people.*

Unique: Create unique ways to do things.
* ❖ *A unique way is new in all respects.*

Unite: Unite people into a group with a common focus.
* ❖ *Unity creates·energy for progress toward a common purpose.*

Uphold: Uphold your principles under all circumstances.
* ❖ *To uphold is to defend against attacks.*

Uplift: Uplift those around you.
* ❖ *To uplift is to improve conditions.*

Useful: Be useful in your community.
* ❖ *Being useful is sharing your abilities in the interest of the community.*

V

Vacation: Take a vacation from time to time.
- ❖ *A vacation nourishes body, mind, and soul.*

Valour: Demonstrate valour when facing threats.
- ❖ *Valour is fearlessness in dangerous situations.*

Valuable: Protect that which you value.
- ❖ *Your valuable assets are physical, mental, and spiritual.*

Venerate: Venerate those for whom you have great admiration.
- ❖ *Veneration is a mark of respect for a person of high esteem.*

Veracious: Be veracious in everything you say.
- ❖ *Veracity is the absolute truth.*

Versatile: Be versatile in order to overcome setbacks.
- ❖ *Versatility is adaptability when handling problems.*

Viability: Ensure the viability of your projects.

❖ *Viability is the practical possibilities for success.*

Victorious: Be victorious in your fight against the destruction of hope.

❖ *Victory comes from steadfast toughness.*

Vigilant: Be vigilant of factors working against your endeavours.

❖ *To be vigilant is to watch for obstacles in your way.*

Vigour: Employ vigour in your endeavours.

❖ *Vigour is combined vitality, strength, and energy.*

Vindicate: Vindicate a wrong done to you.

❖ *Vindication is the satisfaction that a wrong has been corrected.*

Virtue: Be a person of virtue.

❖ *Virtues form the basis of goodness.*

Vision: Always have a vision to follow.
❖ *A vision is the focal point of guidance.*

Vitality: Strive towards continuous vitality by caring for your body, mind, and spirit.
❖ *Vitality is essential for success.*

Vivacious: Be vivacious as a way of life.
❖ *To be vivacious is to be cheerful and spirited.*

Vivid: Develop a vivid memory.
❖ *A vivid memory is a useful source of knowledge.*

Vivify: Vivify new projects with enthusiasm.
❖ *To vivify is to put life into something.*

Volunteer: Volunteer to be of service to the community.
❖ *Volunteering is an opportunity to serve the community.*

W

Warmth: Radiate warmth toward your loved ones.
* ❖ *Warmth heals and binds people together.*

Wealth: Dream and work, and wealth will follow.
* ❖ *Wealth is measured in money, family, friends, contributions, and the distribution of goodness.*

Welfare: Keep the welfare of your community at heart.
* ❖ *The welfare of the community is everybody's responsibility.*

Wellbeing: Care about your wellbeing.
* ❖ *Your wellbeing is dependent on your own endeavours.*

Whole: Strive to be a whole person.
* ❖ *A whole person is always interested in the bigger picture.*

Wholehearted: Embark whole-heartedly into your project.
❖ *A wholehearted approach involves doing something with all you have.*

Wholesome: Nourish your body with wholesome meals.
❖ *A wholesome meal helps to keep you healthy.*

Will: Exercise your will to overcome.
❖ *To say 'I will' is more powerful than saying 'I can.'*

Willing: Be willing to serve.
❖ *To be willing to go out of your way to help is admirable.*

Win: Win victories over your obstacles.
❖ *To win is to be victorious.*

Winsome: Be a winsome person.
❖ *A winsome person is engaging and pleasing.*

Wisdom: Lead with wisdom.
❖ *Wisdom is the combination of knowledge, experience, and common sense.*

Worship: Worship God, who has given you talents.

❖ *To worship is to pay homage to the Almighty.*

X

No positive words

Y

Yearn: Yearn for even more goodness in all people.
❖ *Yearning is the ultimate of hoping.*

Yes: Say 'Yes' to that which is good.
❖ *A 'Yes' for what is good is a rejection of that which is bad.*

Young: Be young at heart.
❖ *To be young at heart is to retain your youthfulness.*

Z

Zeal: Follow your goals with zeal.
* ❖ *To have zeal is to be enthusiastic and keen.*

Zealous: Be zealous when tackling a task.
* ❖ *To be zealous is to be eager and enthusiastic.*

Zest: Display zest in your everyday life.
* ❖ *To have zest is to have a love for life.*

INDEX

The Index is organized to correspond to the five basic elements of positive living and to the Positive Pledge, as shown in brackets below, at the beginning of the book.

If you are looking for a word to help you with a specific situation, go to the topic that best relates to your situation.

Basic values (I will abide by the good values I have accepted.)

Spiritual values (I will foster my spiritual life.)

Almighty, Depend, Laud, Pray, Worship.

Positive outlook (I will be positive as a way of life.)

Abolish, Abstain, Advance, Advocate, Affect, Agree, Alleviate, Amend, Ardent, Assert, Attitude, Certainty, Commit, Confirm, Connect, Consider, Consistent, Convalesce, Covenant, Curtail, Defeat, Demonstrate, Denounce, Desire, Develop, Discourse, Distinguish, Earnest, Elect, Eliminate, Elude, Emotion, Enact, Endeavour, Endorse, Enterprise, Eradicate, Exert, Fabulous, Form, Function, Gather, Habit, Impress, Increase, Induce, Instil, Jubilant, Live, Look, Love, Negotiate, Obtain, Passionate, Penchant, Persuade, Positive, Propagate, Pursue, Raise, Reap, Recommend, Reduce, Represent, Resolve, Revere, Shape, Spread, Sunny, Teach.

Goodness (I will foster goodness.)

Accede, Admire, Adore, Alliance, Ambition, Applaud, Approve, Bountiful, Celebrate, Cheerful, Conscious, Debate, Deed, Defend, Desist, Differentiate, Dignify, Discern, Discretion, Ensure, Exalt, Good, Goodwill, Hope, Increase, Influence, Inform, Joyful, Lasting, Open, Propitious, Recognize, Relentless, Requite, Retain, Retrieve, Sacrifice, Side, Spirit, Suggest, Sustain, Yearn, Yes.

Thinking (I will be pure and rational in my thinking.)

Appraise, Cogitate, Comprehend, Conceive, Concentrate, Conscience, Consider, Contemplate, Convalesce, Create, Decide, Deliberate, Devise, Establish, Evolve, Examine, Holistic, Imagine, Ingenious, Innovate, Meditate, Memory, Memorize, Mind, Original, Pensive, Pure, Rational, Recollect, Remember, Self-control, Sensible, Sound, Thoughtful, Understand, Unique, Vivid.

Enjoyment (I will enjoy the many good things in life.)

Aesthetic, Allot, Amuse, Arise, Beam, Beautify, Bloom, Bountiful, Cheerful, Cherish, Curious, Delectable, Delicious, Delight, Derive, Discover, Enchanting, Enjoy, Enrapture, Exuberance, Exult, Fabulous, Fascinate, Fun, Hearty, Homey, Humour, Joyful, Jubilant, Lasting, Laugh, Love, Magnificent, Marvellous, Merriment, Observe, Overjoyed, Peaceful, Pleasure, Precious, Quiet, Rapture, Recollect, Recreate, Rejoice, Rejuvenate, Relax, Relish, Repose, Restful, Restore, Revel, Rollick, Sentimental, Solitude, Sunny, Terrific, Vacation, Vivacious.

Health and Wellness (I will care for my health and wellness.)

Forbear, Health, Invigorate, Salubrious, Wellbeing, Wholesome.

Courage (I will be courageous.)

Adventurous, Bold, Brave, Courage,
Dare, Face, Hardy, Heroic, Intrepid,
Inure, Invincible, Mettle, Persevere,
Refresh, Stamina, Stoic, Strong, Survive,
Valour, Victorious, Win.

Relationships (I will be compassionate in my relationships.)

Absolve, Accessible, Accommodate,
Acknowledge, Admire, Adore, Advise,
Affable, Affection, Affiliate, Allay,
Allure, Altruistic, Amiable, Apologise,
Appearance, Appease, Appreciate,
Approbation, Assure, Atone, Attentive,
Attract, Avow, Award, Becoming,
Befriend, Benevolent, Benign, Character,
Charm, Cherish, Civil, Clean,
Commemorate, Commend, Compassion,
Compensate, Comport, Conciliate,
Concord, Concur, Condolence,
Condone, Conduct, Confront, Congenial,
Congratulate, Connect, Console,
Consonance, Consult, Cordial, Correct,
Courteous, Credibility, Debate, Decent,
Defray, Defy, Devote, Diplomatic,

Discourse, Durable, Effect, Elate, Elevate, Embolden, Empathy, Enchanting, Endear, Endue, Enlarge, Enlighten, Entrust, Esteem, Exert, Extol, Fair, Felicitate, Gentle, Give, Goodwill, Grace, Grateful, Gratuity, Gregarious, Harmony, Help, Homage, Homey, Humble, Impartial, Influence, Judgment, Judicious, Just, Kind, Lead, Lenient, Lighten, Manners, Mediate, Mild, Mitigate, Moderate, Natty, Neat, Oblige, Ovation, Pacify, Pay, Perceive, Persuade, Pleasant, Please, Polished, Posture, Praise, Present, Presentable, Privilege, Profuse, Promise, Proper, Reasonable, Reassure, Receive, Reciprocate, Recognize, Reconcile, Rectify, Redeem, Redress, Refine, Regard, Rehabilitate, Relieve, Rely, Renew, Repay, Repent, Respectable, Respectful, Restrain, Reward, Salutation, Salve, Self-possessed, Self-restraint, Self-sacrifice, Sensitive, Shield, Sincere, Solace, Soothe, Sorry, Special, Staunch, Surprise, Sympathy, Tact, Temperance, Tender, Thoughtful, Tolerate, Treat, Tribute, Truce, Trust, Understand, Unite, Venerate, Vindicate, Warmth, Willing, Winsome, Wisdom.

Work (I will work diligently to get the best possible results.)

Able, Ability, Aboveboard, Accurate, Actuate, Acumen, Acute, Adept, Adequate, Adjust, Adopt, Amenable, Anticipate, Attention, Capable, Captivate, Cogent, Compatible, Concord, Consider, Construct, Consult, Delegate, Deserve, Devout, Dexterous, Do, Earn, Embark, Endue, Enough, Enterprise, Entrust, Exact, Forecast, Fresh, Harmony, Illuminate, Impeccable, Improve, Ingenious, Initiate, Innovate, Instinct, Integrate, Launch, Meditate, Memorize, Meticulous, Outcome, Pensive, Plan, Plausible, Pleasant, Ply, Pragmatic, Prolific, Quality, Ready, Reconsider, Reform, Rehearse, Reinforce, Reliable, Rely, Reorganize, Result, Revise, Sedulous, Studious, Suggest, Thrive, Transform, Truce, Viability, Wealth, Wholehearted, Wisdom.

Effectiveness (I will be effective in whatever I do.)

Able, Accurate, Attention, Circumspection, Clarity, Cogent, Compatible, Competence, Compose, Concise, Conscientious, Construct, Contingency, Cope, Cultivate, Effective, Efficient, Emulate, Enable, Enough, Exact, Examine, Exceed, Excel, Excellent, Exemplify, Facilitate, Finish, Forecast, Foresee, Form, Frugal, Guarantee, Handy, Illuminate, Instinct, Integrate, Lucid, Maintain, Merit, Optimum, Organize, Outcome, Output, Partnership, Perform, Plausible, Practical, Prepare, Proactive, Proficient, Prosper, Provide, Prowess, Prudent, Punctual, Ready, Reason, Reconsider, Rehabilitate, Rehearse, Reinforce, Renovate, Reorganize, Repair, Replenish, Resourceful, Sagacious, Save, Self-confidence, Self-reliant, Self-supporting, Skilful, Solve, Splendid, Standard, Sufficient, Sure, Surplus, Swift, Temperance, Thorough, Thrifty, Transform, Versatile, Vigilant, Victorious.

Goals (I will work to attain the goals I have set.)

Able, Absolute, Accept, Achieve, Act, Adhere, Aim, Apply, Aptitude, Ascend, Assiduous, Attain, Auspicious, Believe, Conduce, Confident, Cooperate, Determination, Enable, Exceed, Exult, Follow, Ideal, Labour, Make, Mission, Navigate, Noteworthy, Outdo, Outset, Overcome, Partnership, Passionate, Persist, Praiseworthy, Procure, Produce, Progress, Prolific, Purpose, Quest, Realize, Regenerate, Remarkable, Resolute, Revive, Rise, Romance, Standard, Splendid, Steady, Stimulate, Strive, Success, Superlative, Surpass, Talent, Toughen, Transcendent, Vision, Whole , Zeal.

Learning (I will continue to learn.)

Ability, Able, Accumulate, Abreast, Absorb, Acquaint, Acquire, Aggregate, Amass, Competence, Cultivate, Edify, Educate, Empower, Enlighten, Interest, Know, Knowledge, Learn, Memorize, Memory, Observe, Open, Peruse,

Qualify, Rediscover, Scholar, Sound, Study.

Motivation (I will be motivated in everything I do.)

Alacrity, Animate, Arise, Begin, Brisk, Calm, Can, Commence, Conquer, Curious, Debonair, Ease, Effervesce, Elevate, Embolden, Encourage, Endeavour, Energy, Enliven, Enthusiasm, Evoke, Excite, Faith, Fresh, Gusto, Incentive, Induce, Influence, Infuse, Inspire, Invigorate, Keen, Kindle, Launch, Lively, Look, Morale, Motivate, Prevail, Rebound, Recover, Reduce, Self-confidence, Spirited, Spring, Spry, Stalwart, Tackle, Trust, Uplift, Vigour, Vitality, Vivify, Wholehearted, Will, Young, Zeal, Zealous, Zest.

Community Service (I will serve my community.)

Acquiesce, Astute, Avail, Benefactor, Benefit, Benevolent, Care, Charitable, Cognizant, Contribute, Dedicate, Donate, Drive, Eager, Endow, Engage, Enhance, Example, Further, Help, Heritage, Invest,

Involve, Noble, Oblige, Opportunity, Patron, Philanthropic, Promote, Propitious, Render, Serve, Stalwart, Useful, Volunteer, Welfare, Willing.

Diane,

Sometimes just changing our thoughts makes things brighter...

Love
monica

Dec 2006